Soccer Superstars 2017

TRIUMPH
B O O K S

Contents

"Agüero is every bit as important to [Man City] as Luis Suárez was to Liverpool last year or Gareth Bale to Tottenham Hotspur the year before."

—English soccer journalist Martin Samuel

Sergio Agüero

Hometown:
Buenos Aires, Argentina
Club: Manchester City

Known to all by his nickname "Kun," Agüero has been compared to Brazilian soccer legend Romário, as well as his former father-in-law, Diego Maradona. After scoring five goals for Man City in just 20 minutes in a match against Newcastle early in the 2015–2016 season, there may soon be no one left to compare Kun to.

Raised in modest circumstances, Agüero became the youngest player to appear in a match for Independiente at the age of 15 in 2003. In 2005–2006 he scored 18 goals in just 36 games and was quickly scooped up by La Liga club Atlético Madrid, where he spent five seasons, quickly becoming Atlético's top offensive threat, scoring 101 goals in 234 matches.

Agüero joined Manchester City in 2011 for a Sky Blues record transfer fee of £35 million. His impact was felt immediately, as he shined in his debut, scoring an assist and two goals. But it was in the final match of the season that Agüero became a local legend. His goal in the 95th minute gave Man City its first Premier League title and its first top-division trophy since 1968. City of Manchester Stadium erupted as Agüero's teammates mobbed him on the field. Another league title followed in 2013–2014, along with a League Cup.

Agüero won a Gold Medal with Argentina in the 2008 Olympics. Teamed with Lionel Messi again for the 2014 World Cup, Argentina finished as runners-up to Germany. A young, stout striker who plays with strength, agility, and speed, Kun Agüero looks to be getting better and should be a force for years to come.

Fast Stat:

5

Goals Kun scored in 20 minutes vs. Newcastle on October 3, 2015

Ht: 5'8" • **Wt:** 170 • **DOB:** 6/2/88

Position: Striker

2015–2016 salary:
$14.7 million

Career goals/International caps:
271 goals/79 caps

Personal homepage:
http://www.sergioaguero.com/EN

Twitter: @aguerosergiokun

Did you know? A tattoo on Kun's right arm is written in Elvish, the Middle Earth language J.R.R. Tolkien invented for *The Lord of the Rings*.

As a kid: He liked to repeat the name "Kum Kum" from his favorite cartoon (as "Kun Kun"), so a family friend dubbed him "Kun."

Favorite foods: Argentine beef and pasta (both of which Kun had to cut from his diet to avoid injury)

Hobbies: Making defenders look foolish and hanging with Argentina national teammate Lionel Messi

Favorite music: Cumbia (Kun sang on Los Leales' song "El Kun Agüero")

Marco Reus

Hometown: Dortmund, Germany
Club: Borussia Dortmund

Known for his speed, versatility, and technique, Marco Reus has become an offensive star of the Bundesliga, where he has spent his club career, and since 2010 as a member and then starter for the eventual World Cup–champion German national team.

Joining the youth program of his hometown Borussia Dortmund club at the age of seven, Reus spent 10 years coming up through Dortmund's ranks. But Dortmund let him go in 2006 to play for the U-19 team of Rot Weiss Ahlen, where he broke into the first team within a year. By 2008–2009 he was a mainstay, playing in 27 matches and scoring four goals. This led to his signing with Bundesliga club Borussia Mönchengladbach, where he would become a prolific goalscorer, netting 41 goals over three seasons. At the end of the 2011–2012 season, Reus was named the Footballer of the Year in Germany. His old club took notice.

Signing Reus away for a $19.6 million transfer fee, Borussia Dortmund reclaimed the hometown midfielder before the start of the 2012–2013 season. He scored a goal in his August debut with Dortmund and then two more for a brace against his former team in September. Reus and teammate Mario Götze soon became one of the most dangerous midfield duos in soccer, until Götze left for Bayern Munich in 2013. Reus has scored 62 goals with Dortmund since rejoining the team, including six in his first six games of 2015. He has helped Dortmund to two DFL-Supercups and was named the Dortmund Player of the Year for 2013–2014 as well as being named to the Champions League Team of the Season.

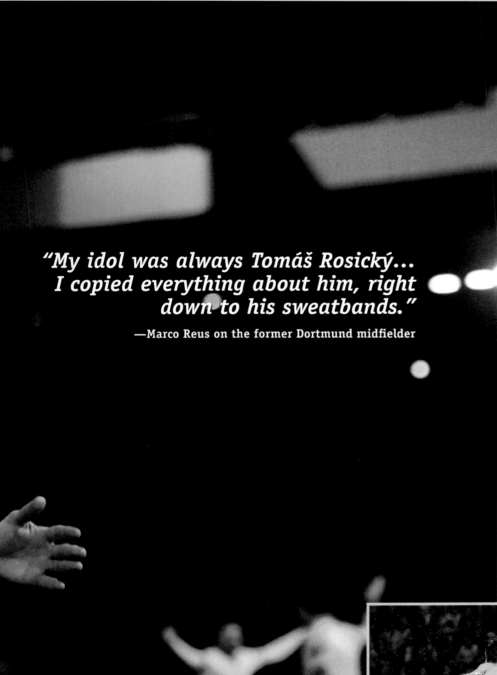

"My idol was always Tomáš Rosický... I copied everything about him, right down to his sweatbands."

—Marco Reus on the former Dortmund midfielder

Fast Stat:

53

Goals scored by Marco in his first three seasons with Borussia Dortmund

Ht: 5'11" • **Wt:** 148 • **DOB:** 5/31/89

Position: Midfield/Winger

2015–2016 salary:
$4.5 million

Career club goals/International caps:
125 goals/29 caps

Twitter: @woodyinho

Did you know? German newspaper *Bild* nicknamed Marco "Rolls Reus."

Fun tidbit: One of the tattoos on Marco's left arm is a quote by Oprah, which reads, "The biggest adventure you can take is to live your Dreams."

As a kid: Marco began playing for his hometown club Post SV Dortmund at the age of five.

Favorite foods: Mashed potatoes, goulash, and cabbage

Hobbies: Ping-Pong and video games (especially EA Sport's FIFA series)

Favorite music: R&B and hip-hop, Lena, and Justin Bieber

Cristiano Ronaldo

Hometown:
Funchal, Madeira, Portugal
Club: Real Madrid

Fast Stat:

6

Number of consecutive seasons with 50 or more goals, an unmatched record

Ht: 6′1″ • **Wt:** 180 • **DOB:** 2/5/85

Position: Forward

2015–2016 salary:
$35.9 million

Career club goals/International caps:
491 goals/135 caps

Personal homepage:
http://www.cristianoronaldo.com

Twitter: @Cristiano

Did you know? At 15 Ronaldo was diagnosed with a career-threatening heart condition that required surgery to repair.

As a kid: Ronaldo grew up on the island of Madeira, where at the age of eight he joined the amateur team Andorinha, where his father was the kit man.

Fun tidbit: Ronaldo, who goes by his second given name, was named after Ronald Reagan, his father's favorite actor.

Favorite foods: Bacalhau à Brás (a traditional Portuguese dish of salted cod, potatoes, onions, and eggs)

Hobbies: Cars, fashion, and charity

Favorite music: Elton John, Phil Collins, and Brazilian music

If any debate remains as to whether Lionel Messi is the best soccer player in the world, it revolves around Cristiano Ronaldo, the Portuguese superstar who spent six seasons with Manchester United before joining Real Madrid, the archrival of Messi's Barcelona club. Winning the FIFA Ballon d'Or for 2013–2014 and 2014–2015, Ronaldo has only added fuel to the fire over the title of best player of his generation.

What isn't debatable is Ronaldo's claim as being one of the greatest footballers in the history of the sport. His professional career began at the age of 16 with Sporting CP in Lisbon, where he became the only player to ever advance from the under-16 team to first team in one season. It didn't take long for English powerhouse Manchester United to take notice, and they signed Ronaldo for £12.24 million in 2003.

Given the No. 7 shirt worn by David Beckham, Ronaldo quickly lived up to expectations. During 2007–2008, he scored 31 goals for Man U, helping his team to their second of three straight Premier League championships and his first Ballon d'Or. Ronaldo also excelled for the Portugal national team, being named permanent captain in July 2008 and helping Portugal to the UEFA Euro 2016 championship.

Moving to his current team, Real Madrid, in 2009, Ronaldo became its leading goalscorer of all-time in only six-plus seasons and led Madrid to a league title in 2011–2012. In 2015 he became the only player to ever win four European Golden Shoe awards and was named the best Portuguese player of all-time by the Portuguese Football Federation.

"If Messi is the best on the planet, Ronaldo is the best in the universe."

—Former Real Madrid manager
José Mourinho

"Five goals! Neither as a coach nor as a player did I ever experience something like this."

—Bayern manager Pep Guardiola on Lewandowski scoring five goals in under nine minutes against Wolfsburg

Robert Lewandowski

Hometown: Warsaw, Poland
Club: Bayern Munich

Scoring in bunches is nothing unusual for Polish striker Robert Lewandowski, who collected five braces and a pair of hat-tricks in just his second Bundesliga season (2011–2012), leading all scorers in the DFB-Pokal tournament for Borussia Dortmund. In April 2013 he became the first player to score four goals in a Champions League semifinal, versus Real Madrid. Lewandowski collected another hat-trick for Dortmund in 2013–2014 and then netted a couple of braces in his first season with former rival Bayern Munich (2014–2015). But on September 22, 2015, Lewandowski outdid himself and every other Bundesliga player ever: coming on as a substitute while trailing Wolfsburg 1–0, he scored five goals in under nine minutes to lift Bayern to a 5–1 victory.

He then scored a hat-trick a week later in a Champions League win over Dinamo Zagreb and two more goals five days later against Dortmund.

Lewandowski seems to rise to top goal-scorer of whatever league he's playing in. Having led the top three flights of Polish soccer in scoring, he joined Dortmund in 2010 and promptly won two league titles before switching to archrival Bayern, where he led the league in scoring in 2013–2014 and became the fastest foreign player in Bundesliga history to reach 100 goals.

One of the top goalscorers in the world, Lewandowski has played for the Polish national team since he was 20 years old and became captain in 2013. In 2014–2015 he scored two hat-tricks, a brace, and headed in the winner against Ireland on October 8, 2015, to qualify Poland for the finals of the UEFA Euro 2016 tournament.

Fast Stat:

42

Goals Robert scored overall in 2015–2016 with Bayern Munich, a career best

Ht: 6'0" • **Wt:** 172 • **DOB:** 8/21/88

Position: Striker

2015–2016 salary:
$11.2 million

Career club goals/International caps:
258 goals/84 caps

Personal homepage:
http://lewandowskiofficial.com

Twitter: @lewy_official

Did you know? A practicing Catholic, Robert got to meet Pope Francis after Bayern Munich beat AS Roma 7–1 in a Champions League match in 2014.

As a kid: Robert grew up in a very athletic household—his mother is a former pro volleyball player, and his father was a Polish judo champion and soccer player.

Hobbies: Following basketball and boxing

Favorite music: Jay Z

Andrés Iniesta

Hometown: Fuentealbilla, Spain
Club: FC Barcelona

One of the greatest all-around players of the last 12 years and probably one of the greatest midfielders of all-time, Barcelona captain Andrés Iniesta has been an integral part of championship squads for both Barça and Spain's national team.

Born and raised in a small village in the southeast of the Castile–La Mancha region of Spain, Iniesta was recruited at the age of 12 to join FC Barcelona's youth academy. Though homesick and shy around the older soccer prodigies, Iniesta captained Barça's Under-15 team to victory in the Nike Premier Cup in 1999. He debuted for the first team at the age of 18 in 2002, began playing regularly in 2004, and has never stopped.

Iniesta was instrumental in helping Barça to a record six trophies in 2009, the year he was named La Liga Spanish Player of the Year. A critical part of a Barcelona team that has won eight league championships, four Copa del Reys, four Champions League titles, and two FIFA Club World Cups, Iniesta has also earned numerous individual awards, including the 2014 Golden Foot and 2012 UEFA Best Player in Europe Award.

After helping its Under-16 and Under-19 teams to European Championships, Iniesta made Spain's national team in 2006. Spain won the UEFA Euro 2008 with Iniesta named to the Team of the Tournament. Then, in the 2010 World Cup, Spain reached the final against The Netherlands after three 1–0 wins. In the 116th minute of the game, Iniesta netted the game-winner to give Spain another 1–0 win and its first-ever World Championship. His entire career spent in Spain, Iniesta is without a doubt one of the best Spaniards of all-time.

"The one who plays this game the best is Iniesta... He picks the right moment to do everything: when to dribble, when to speed things up, and when to slow things down."

—Former Argentinian great
Juan Román Riquelme

Fast Stat:

1

Number of clubs Iniesta has played for in his career

Ht: 5′7″ • **Wt:** 143 • **DOB:** 5/11/84

Position: Midfield

2015–2016 salary:
$5.6 million

Career club goals/International caps:
55 goals/111 caps

Twitter: @andresiniesta8

Did you know? Andrés earned a yellow card after his 2010 World Cup–winning goal for taking off his jersey, which revealed a handwritten message on his undershirt in tribute to late teammate Dani Jarque.

As a kid: Andrés' father saved for three months to be able to buy him a pair of Adidas Predator boots.

Favorite foods: Chicken with potatoes

Hobbies: Harvesting grapes at the family vineyard, listening to music, spending time with family

Favorite music: English indie rock band Kasabian and Spanish rock/ rumba duo Estopa

Mesut Özil

Hometown:
Gelsenkirchen, Germany
Club: Arsenal

Ht: 5'11" • **Wt:** 168 • **DOB:** 10/15/88

Position: Midfield

2015–2016 salary:
$9.4 million

Career club goals/International caps:
71 goals/83 caps

Twitter: @MesutOzil1088

Did you know? With Arsenal's club-record transfer fee of £42.5 million, Mesut became the most expensive German footballer of all-time.

Fun Fact: Özil donated his 2014 World Cup winnings, an estimated $306,000, to pay for 23 sick Brazilian kids to have surgery as a "personal thank you for the hospitality of the people of Brazil."

As a kid: Mesut developed his soccer skills while playing with friends in the "Monkey Cage," a local field enclosed by fences.

Favorite foods: Kebabs; and ice cream, which is unfortunate as Mesut is lactose-intolerant.

Hobbies: In keeping with Mesut's uncany ability to anticipate what's going to happen on the field, his favorite game away from it is chess.

Favorite music: Rap, Wiz Khalifa

Known for his ability to set up his teammates for goalscoring opportunities, Mesut Özil broke out in the 2010 World Cup as a 21-year-old midfielder for the German national team. He was nominated for the Golden Ball, awarded to the tournament's best all-around player. Soon Real Madrid came calling, and Özil's career took off.

An attacking midfielder who tends to improvise on the pitch and play with finesse, Özil has been compared to Real Madrid legend Zinedine Zidane for his style and assist-making skills.

Of Turkish descent, Özil was born and raised in Gelsenkirchen, Germany, where he began his youth career before moving to Rot-Weiss Essen at the age of 12. In 2005 he transferred to Bundesliga mainstay Schalke 04, where he first broke onto the first team, playing two seasons there and then two years with German rival Werder Bremen.

Although he could have played for Turkey, Özil, a third-generation German, never doubted that he'd play for the country of his birth. Making the German team in 2009, he shone in Germany's 2010 third-place World Cup finish and was crucial in the team's 2014 World Cup title.

After establishing himself as a bona fide star with Real Madrid from 2010–2013—leading La Liga in assists all three seasons and being shortlisted for the Ballon D'or—Özil moved to the Premier League and Arsenal for a club-record transfer fee, where he has become an integral part of one of the top teams in the league, continuing to rack up assists, goals, and wins.

"Özil is unique. There is no copy of him—not even a bad copy."

— Former Real Madrid manager
José Mourinho

Paul Pogba

Hometown:
Lagny-sur-Marne, France
Club: Manchester United

Named by the *Guardian* as one of the 10 most promising young players in Europe in January 2014, Paul Pogba has gone on to exceed those lofty expectations. He helped Turin-based Juventus to three straight Serie A league titles and was honored after leading team France to the quarterfinals of the 2014 World Cup as the tournament's Best Young Player. Pogba, nicknamed *Il Polpo Paul* ("Paul the Octopus") and "Pogboom" by Italian fans, is just 23 and promises to become even better. On August 8, 2016, Pogba returned to Manchester United for an all-time record transfer fee of $114.6 million.

Pogba began his youth career in France but showed so much talent he was poached by Manchester United in 2009 at the age of 16, much to the dismay of his former team, Le Havre. After two years on the under-18 team and a frustrating season with the first team, however, Pogba left Man U for Italy and Juventus, where he blossomed. Pogba helped lead Juventus' resurgence, playing with explosive energy and power, able to score goals from almost anywhere on the pitch. In addition to his club's success, Pogba received the Golden Boy award in 2013 (for best under-21 player in Europe) and the Bravo Award in 2014 (best under-21). In 2015 he was named to the 10-man shortlist for the Best Player in Europe Award. Whether it's finding the net from 40 yards out or making mind-boggling moves with the dribble, Pogba has a penchant for the spectacular.

Already a force on France's national team after two years, Pogba said his wish is to compete against his twin older brothers in a match against Guinea.

"People compare us, but where I would win more tackles, Paul is more technically gifted than I ever was... He can be one of the best in the world."

—Patrick Vieira

Fast Stat:

4

Number of goals Paul scored with France in 2014, the year of his first World Cup

Ht: 6'2" • **Wt:** 176 • **DOB:** 3/15/93

Position: Midfield

2015–2016 salary:
$19.4 million

Career club goals/International caps:
37 goals/42 caps

Twitter: @paulpogba

Did you know? Paul has twin older brothers, Florentin and Mathias, who also play pro soccer in Europe, but are members of the Guinea national team. Unlike Paul, who was born in France, they were born in Guinea.

As a kid: Paul began his soccer career at the age of six with US Roissy-en-Brie, near his hometown, where he played for seven seasons before moving to US Torcy.

Favorite foods: Pasta with chicken and salmon with potatoes

Hobbies: Travel, playing video games, and watching basketball

Favorite music: Jay Z and Kanye West

Lionel Messi

Hometown: Rosario, Argentina
Club: FC Barcelona

Bursting onto the international soccer scene in 2004 as a 17-year-old, Leo Messi's status as the world's best footballer has become consensus. The only question remaining for the player often compared to Pelé and fellow Argentinian Diego Maradona, is whether he will surpass (or has already surpassed) those two legends.

At the age of 11, a growth hormone deficiency nearly derailed his career, but an offer from FC Barcelona to cover his treatments and play at their youth academy in 2000 brought Messi to Spain to stay. It proved to be an insanely good investment for Barcelona, as Messi soon climbed the ranks of Barça's junior teams.

Messi made his La Liga debut on October 16, 2004, and quickly became a starter and star for one of Europe's top teams, helping Barça to eight league titles in 12 seasons. Displaying unmatched ball-handling skills, Messi weaves around and often through defenders as if the ball were attached to his foot by an invisible string—until he launches it into the back of the opponents' net. The leading scorer in La Liga history, he also holds the league assist record.

In 2014–2015 Messi scored 58 goals while leading Barça to its second treble— winning La Liga, the Copa del Rey, and the Champions League in one season—while winning the UEFA Best Player in Europe award for the second time. He also captained the Argentina national team to a runner-up finish in the 2014 World Cup, where he earned the Golden Ball as the tournament's best player. Messi is the only player to win four Ballons d'Or and the first to win three European Golden Shoes.

Fast Stat:
91
Record number of goals Leo scored for Barcelona and Argentina in 2012

Ht: 5'6" • **Wt:** 148 • **DOB:** 6/24/87

Position: Striker

2015–2016 salary:
$44.9 million

Career club goals/International caps:
467 goals/114 caps

Twitter: @_10_lionelmessi

Did you know? Leo is left-footed, and most of his goals are struck by his prodigious left foot.

As a kid: From the age of six to 12, Leo scored nearly 500 goals for Newell's Old Boys, his youth team in Rosario, Argentina.

Favorite foods: Milanesa Napolitana

Hobbies: Playing guitar and spending time with his partner, Antonella Roccuzzo, and their two sons, Thiago and Mateo

Favorite music: Cumbia, reggae

"Messi is an alien who dedicates himself to playing with humans."

—Juventus captain Gianluigi Buffon

Gareth Bale

Hometown: Cardiff, Wales
Club: Real Madrid

Growing up idolizing fellow Welshman pro footballer Ryan Giggs, Gareth Bale was discovered by Southampton at the tender age of nine on his local school team. He made his professional and international debut at the age of 16 in 2006 and was shortly after snapped up by Tottenham Hotspur of the Premier League in 2007.

Though he scored goals against Fulham, Arsenal, and Middlesbrough, Bale endured a winless streak of 24 games across two-plus years to start his tenure with the Spurs, which also saw him suffer a serious injury to his right ankle. After another injury in 2009, Bale returned to the pitch and showed signs of brilliance in his first wins for Tottenham and was named Player of the Month for April 2010.

In 2010–2011 Bale moved from midfield to left wing and became more of an offensive force over the next three seasons, scoring 49 goals.

In 2013 Real Madrid paid a then record transfer fee of £85.3 million to secure Bale's services. Joining Cristiano Ronaldo, Bale contributed key goals in Real Madrid's victories in both the Champions League and Copa del Rey in 2013–2014.

The youngest player to ever score a goal for the Welsh national team, Bale has 54 caps with Wales and 19 goals, making him Wales' sixth-highest scorer of all-time.

One of the fastest players in the world (he could run the 100m in 11.4 seconds at age 14), Bale wears down defenders with his speed and stamina. Also known as a free-kick specialist, Bale's powerful, swerving kicks earned him the nickname "The Cannon" from the Spanish press.

"He made me feel an inch tall. Took me to pieces. He just doesn't stop running. It's ridiculous."

—Manchester City fullback Micah Richards

Fast Stat:

16

Bale's age when he made his professional debut with Southampton in 2006

Ht: 6'0" • **Wt:** 163 • **DOB:** 7/16/89

Position: Midfield/Winger

2015–2016 salary: $19.3 million

Career club goals/International caps: 122 goals/64 caps

Twitter: @GarethBale11

Did you know? Gareth doesn't drink alcohol. He doesn't care for the taste.

As a kid: During school games, Gareth's coach wouldn't allow him to use his left foot, so as to give the other kids a chance.

Fun tidbit: Gareth had his "heart hands" goal celebration trademarked in 2013.

Favorite foods: Corned beef hash

Hobbies: Hockey, rugby, track & field

Favorite music: Brian McFadden

Christian Pulisic

Hometown:
Hershey, Pennsylvania
Club: Borussia Dortmund

Having risen faster and higher than any other American player in history, Christian Pulisic is making believers of fans who've waited a long time for a U.S. soccer star to rival those from Europe and Latin America.

Having turned just 18 in September 2016, Pulisic is already a starter on the U.S. soccer squad and a solid contributor on one of Germany's top professional teams, Borussia Dortmund. In April 2016, he became the youngest foreigner to ever score in the Bundesliga, and a week later he became the youngest player of any nationality to score two goals in the league. Still before his 18th birthday, he would also become the youngest player in the modern era to score a goal for the U.S. and then netted two goals in a 2018 World Cup qualification match, making him the youngest American to score a goal in a World Cup Qualifier as well as the youngest to score a brace in U.S. history.

Pulisic grew up in Pennsylvania, the son of a former professional indoor soccer player and coach, and took to the sport at a tender age. After a year spent with a youth team in England at the age of seven, Pulisic played with youth club PA Classics in the Hershey area for seven years before signing with Borussia Dortmund's youth program at the age of 16. In only 15 games with their U19 team, Pulisic scored 10 goals and added another eight assists. Quickly promoted to the first team, he made his Bundesliga debut on January 30, 2016, and started his first match in February. With two more goals just six games into 2016–2017, Pulisic finds himself with prospects other American players could only dream of.

Fast Stat:

17

Age at which Christian started for the U.S. national team and Bundesliga power Borussia Dortmund

Ht: 5'8" • **Wt:** 139 • **DOB:** 9/18/98

Position: Midfield/Winger

2015–2016 salary:
$1.1 million

Career club goals/International caps:
4 goals/9 caps

Twitter: @cpulisic_10

Did you know? With a grandfather from Croatia, Christian secured a Croatian passport to avoid having to apply for a work visa after moving to Germany.

Fun Fact: Christian's cousin Will joined Borussia Dortmund's youth team in March 2016.

As a kid: At the age of seven, Christian spent a year in England and played for the youth team of Brackley Town.

Hobbies: Basketball and Ping-Pong

Favorite music: Justin Bieber

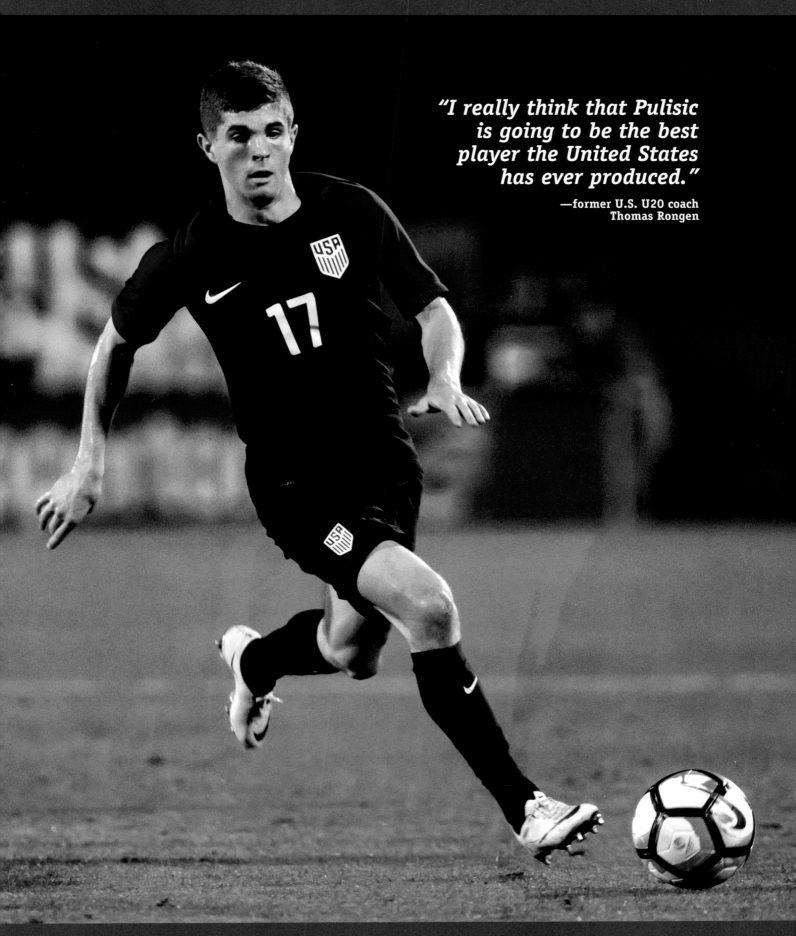

"I really think that Pulisic is going to be the best player the United States has ever produced."

—former U.S. U20 coach
Thomas Rongen

"He is the world's best keeper. At his age I wasn't close to that."

—Oliver Kahn

Manuel Neuer

Hometown:
Gelsenkirchen, Germany
Club: Bayern Munich

Widely regarded as the best and most innovative goalkeeper in soccer today, Manuel Neuer is often described as a "sweeper-keeper," meaning that he roams between the box and the more forward defensive position of sweeper, in order to cut off attackers before they have a clean shot on goal. His size and athleticism also give him incredible shot-stopping ability, and he distributes the ball expertly, many times setting up his mates for scores.

Having come off a 2014 World Cup championship with his German national team in which he allowed a single goal (a late score in Germany's 7–1 rout of host Brazil) and won the Golden Glove as the tournament's best keeper, Neuer is at the top of his game. In September 2016, he was named captain of the German team.

Neuer came up professionally with local team FC Schalke 04 and soon became the starting keeper as a 20-year-old. He was a finalist for the 2007–2008 UEFA Club Goalkeeper of the Year award, the youngest keeper on the list, as well as the only Bundesliga player. By 2011 Bayern Munich bought him for $25 million, to the vocal displeasure of the team's fans, who didn't like buying a rival keeper. Soon enough, they changed their minds, as Neuer broke the Bayern record for consecutive clean sheets and blossomed into the consensus greatest goalkeeper in the game. Neuer helped Bayern to a rare treble in 2012–2013, with four shutouts in a row versus both Juventus and Barça in the Champions League playoffs. Three more Bundesliga titles have followed with Neuer in goal, continuing the Munich team's dominance.

Fast Stat:

20

Clean sheets Manuel posted in 2014–2015 & 2015–2016, a Bundesliga record

Ht: 6'4" • **Wt:** 203 • **DOB:** 3/27/86

Position: Goalkeeper

2015–2016 salary: $7.6 million

Career club saves/International caps: 1,165 saves/71 caps

Twitter: @Manuel_Neuer

Did you know? Manuel voiced the character Frank McCay in the German version of the 2013 Disney Pixar film *Monsters University*.

As a kid: Manuel received his first soccer ball at the age of two and played his first game at four.

Favorite foods: Potato fritters with salmon and salad

Hobbies: Tennis, skiing, watching movies and quiz shows (Manuel won $563,000 for charity on the German version of *Who Wants to Be a Millionaire?*)

Favorite music: Serani, U2

Eden Hazard

Hometown:
Braine-le-Comte, Belgium
Club: Chelsea

Fast Stat:

16

Number of penalties Hazard has made out of 16—the only European to convert all on 15 or more tries

Ht: 5'8" • **Wt:** 163 • **DOB:** 1/7/91

Position: Midfield/Winger

2015–2016 salary:
$13.4 million

Career club goals/International caps:
109 goals/74 caps

Twitter: @hazardeden10

Did you know? Eden is a big basketball fan, his favorite player being the New York Knicks' Carmelo Anthony.

As a kid: Eden lived next to a soccer training ground, where he honed his remarkable skills for hours on end.

Favorite foods: Waffles

Hobbies: Dancing, Ping-Pong

Favorite music: Hip-hop, Beyoncé, The Black Eyed Peas, and French gangsta rappers Booba and Gradur

As the winner of English soccer's three most prestigious honors in 2014–2015—the PFA Players' Player of the Year, FWA Footballer of the Year, and Premier League Player of the Season—Eden Hazard has conquered British football with Premier League and Football League Cup champion Chelsea. And at the age of 24, he's aiming for the crown currently fought over by Lionel Messi and Cristiano Ronaldo.

The son of Belgian soccer players, Hazard began playing for local clubs in his youth before moving to France to join the club academy at Lille. After two years there, he moved up to the first team at the age of 16. Growing into a key member of the team, he would become the first non-French player to win the UNFP Young Player of the Year award in 2008–2009 and the first man to win the award twice after the next season. For 2010–2011 he became the youngest player to win UNFP Ligue 1 Player of the Year honors, while leading his team to league and Coupe de France titles.

Winning Player of the Year with Lille again in 2011–2012, Hazard then signed with Premier League power Chelsea. In his first season, he helped Chelsea to its first ever UEFA Europa League championship and in 2013–2014 was named the PFA Young Player of the Year before his and his team's explosive 2014–2015 season.

Hazard, who also helped his Belgium national squad to the quarterfinals of the 2014 World Cup, is a deft ball-handler who's been compared to Messi. Hazard is also known for his pace, passing, and technical skills. Already one of the best in the world, Hazard is just getting started.

"On his day, nobody can stop him. He has such great quality on the ball. He can create something from nothing, and this is the sign of a special player."

—Thierry Henry

Toni Kroos

Hometown:
Greifswalder, Germany
Club: Real Madrid

Born in the former East Germany, Toni Kroos has the unique distinction of being the only World Cup winner born in the former Soviet satellite. Shortlisted for FIFA's Golden Ball award for the tournament's best player, Kroos scored twice in two minutes in Germany's shocking 7–1 upset seminfinal win over host Brazil and was named man of the match. He also led the tournament in assists and rated as its top player according to the Castrol Performance Index. His standout role in Germany's 2014 World Cup run earned him an offer he couldn't refuse from Real Madrid later that summer, leading him to leave Bayern Munich and the Bundesliga for Spanish La Liga.

A prototypical attacking midfielder, Kroos is known for his vision, passing accuracy, and ability to set up scoring opportunities for teammates. Coming up through his local club team as a youth, Kroos transferred to Bayern Munich's youth program at 16. A year later, in 2007, he was promoted to the senior team, making him the youngest player at the time to ever appear for Bayern in a match, at 17 years, eight months, and two days old. Though Bayern loaned Kroos to rival Bayer Leverkusen for 18 months, he would spend almost five seasons with Munich, becoming one of the best players in Europe, and helping the Bavarians to three league championships, three DFB-Pokal cups, and a Champions League title in 2012–2013.

Since joining Real Madrid, Kroos has gone on to help the Blancos win a UEFA Super Cup, a FIFA Club World Cup, and another Champions League title, while being named to the Champions League Team of the Season three straight years.

> *"How Toni distributes the ball, how he receives it, is very good. He's technically excellent."*
>
> —Joachim Löw,
> manager of the German national team

Fast Stat:

2

Number of clubs with whom Toni has won a Champions League title, the first German player ever to do it

Ht: 6'0" • **Wt:** 172 • **DOB:** 1/4/90

Position: Midfield

2015–2016 salary:
$13.5 million

Career club goals/International caps:
43 goals/74 caps

Twitter: @ToniKroos

Did you know? Toni's younger brother Felix plays midfield for second-division Bundesliga team Union Berlin.

As a kid: A prodigy in soccer, Toni was not the best student in school—perhaps because he missed up to 40 days a year training at soccer.

Favorite foods: Healthy foods rich in protein and carbs, rarely junk food

Hobbies: Playing with his dogs, tennis, and poker

Favorite music: German classic rock

Neymar

Hometown: São Paulo, Brazil
Club: FC Barcelona

Neymar da Silva Santos Jr. drew attention for his stunning soccer skills from an early age in football-crazed Brazil. Joining the youth academy of Santos FC at 11, he was already being courted by European powerhouse Real Madrid by the age of 14. Santos convinced him to stay in Brazil, however, and soon he would star for the senior club.

On March 7, 2009, Neymar made his professional debut for Santos, scoring 14 goals that season in 48 games. Over the next four seasons, he would become a star, scoring 122 goals for Santos and earning numerous awards, including Young Player of the Year in 2011 and South American Footballer of the Year in 2011 and 2012. He would also contribute 46 goals for the Brazil national team in 67 caps and help lead Brazil to the final of the 2012 Olympics against Mexico. In the summer of 2013, he spurred Brazil to victory in the Confederations Cup, scoring a goal in the final versus Spain and being named MVP of the Tournament.

It was just after defeating Spain with his countrymen that Neymar moved across the Atlantic to join Barcelona. In his first season with the star-stacked club, he scored 15 goals in 41 matches. But it was his 2014–2015 season in which he truly broke out, scoring 39 goals, second on Barça only to Lionel Messi. He was the top scorer in the Copa del Rey with seven goals and tied Messi and Cristiano Ronaldo as top goalscorer in the Champions League with 10, both of which Barcelona won. He also played brilliantly for Brazil in the 2014 World Cup before a back injury derailed their run.

A dazzling ball-handler and especially lethal on free kicks, Neymar has explosive scoring ability from anywhere on the pitch.

Fast Stat:

17

Neymar's age when he scored his first professional goal for Santos FC

Ht: 5′9″ • **Wt:** 150 • **DOB:** 2/5/92

Position: Forward/Winger

2015–2016 salary:
$10.3 million

Career club goals/International caps:
227 goals/73 caps

Twitter: @neymarjr

Did you know? His father, Neymar Santos Sr., was also a professional soccer player.

As a kid: Neymar enjoyed playing street football and futsal, a version of indoor soccer.

Favorite foods: Italian, Japanese

Hobbies: Wakeboarding, dancing, and music

Favorite music: Brazilian music, particularly Música sertaneja

"I think...Neymar will become the top goalscorer in Brazil's history, surpassing Pelé."

—Brazil legend Romário

"He is a very unorthodox player... But he has one aim and that is, 'How can I score a goal?'"

—Germany manager Joachim Löw

Thomas Müller

Hometown: Pähl, Germany
Club: Bayern Munich

5

Goals Thomas has scored in each of his first two FIFA World Cups

Ht: 6'1" • **Wt:** 163 • **DOB:** 9/13/89

Position: Midfield/Winger

2015–2016 salary:
$5.6 million

Career club goals/International caps:
155 goals/81 caps

Twitter: @esmuellert_

Did you know? In 2011 he became an ambassador for YoungWings, a charity that helps children who have suffered bereavement or trauma.

As a kid: Thomas began playing soccer on a team in his hometown called TSV Pähl, where Bayern Munich scouts first saw him play.

Favorite foods: Leberkäse sandwich

Hobbies: Golf, cards, breeding horses, and watching his wife Lisa compete in equestrian events

At the 10-minute mark of Germany's 2014 World Cup semifinal match versus Brazil, Thomas Müller scored the opening salvo in the German team's stunning 7–1 rout of their proud Brazilian hosts. It was Müller's fifth goal of the tournament—after his hat-trick against Portugal and the game-winner in Germany's 1–0 win over the U.S. Müller would go on to win the Silver Boot as the 2014 World Cup's second-highest goalscorer (he'd already won the Golden Boot as top scorer in the 2010 World Cup). But more important to Müller, it helped Germany advance to the final, where it defeated Lionel Messi's Argentina team for the world championship and a place in history.

A key member of Bayern Munich, Müller is no stranger to playing on powerhouse championship teams. Born in Weilheim and raised in Pähl, Germany, just outside the Bavarian capital of Munich, Müller entered Bayern's youth system at the age of 10. He debuted on the first team in 2008 at 17 and within a year had worked his way up to a starting position, named the Bundesliga player of the month for September 2009. Capable of playing a variety of forward positions, Müller has been dubbed a *raumdeuter* ("space interpreter") for his ability to find gaps in the defense and exploit them.

Since 2009, he's led his Munich team to five Bundesliga titles, one Champions League title (2012–2013), a UEFA Super Cup (2013), and a FIFA Club World Cup (2013). But, having dominated in the only two FIFA World Cups in which he's played (2010 and 2014) and having led Germany to consecutive third- and first-place finishes, Müller is on a pace to become one of the best ever on soccer's biggest stage.

Alexis Sánchez

Hometown: Tocopilla, Chile
Club: Arsenal

Known to fans simply as Alexis, this Chilean superstar has found a home with north London's Arsenal, fresh off a 2014–2015 campaign that was the best so far of his already impressive career. After netting his 25ᵗʰ goal in Arsenal's 4–0 FA Cup final victory (a dazzling long-range bender that just grazed the bottom of the crossbar), Alexis was rightfully named the club's Player of the Season, among other honors.

Born and raised in the northern Chilean port of Tocopilla, Alexis was promoted to the Cobreloa first team at the age of 16. He quickly caught the attention of Italian club Udinese, which signed him for a $2.6 million fee in 2006 but immediately loaned him out to Chilean club Colo-Colo for maturation. After breaking into the starting lineup and winning a title there, he played in Argentina for a year. Finally, in 2008 Alexis joined Udinese and spent three seasons in Serie A, once scoring four goals in a match against Palermo in 2011.

His 2011 transfer to Barcelona allowed Alexis to play on a team with some of the best players in the world and to compete for titles in La Liga. Despite nagging injuries in his first season with Barça, he scored 15 goals for a team that won a UEFA Super Cup, Copa del Rey, and a FIFA Club World Cup. A league title followed in 2012–2013, and 2013–2014 saw his top goalscoring production to that point, with 21 goals. It was then Arsenal came calling, and Alexis responded with his breakout season, winning PFA Fans' Player of the Year honors.

A quick, energetic offensive force who can create with either foot, Alexis led his Chilean national team to Copa América titles in both 2015 and 2016.

"He's the best signing in the last six years. Arsenal were looking for a player that can deliver on a daily basis—and they have found one."

—Thierry Henry

25

Goals in his first season with Arsenal, most in his career

Ht: 5'7" • **Wt:** 137 • **DOB:** 12/19/88

Position: Winger

2015–2016 salary:
$11.5 million

Career club goals/International caps:
142 goals/101 caps

Twitter: @Alexis_Sanchez

Did you know? His full name is Alexis Alejandro Sánchez Sánchez, but in Chile his nickname is *El Niño Maravilla*, or "The Wonder Boy."

Fun tidbit: Alexis rescued a rabbit (which he later named Alfonso) that had been attacked by a wild boar and nursed it back to health.

As a kid: Alexis played in Cobreloa's youth system, where he was teammates with current national team players Charles Aránguiz and Eduardo Vargas.

Hobbies: Listening to music, browsing the web, social media, and returning home to Chile and his hometown of Tocopilla whenever he can

Favorite music: Niall Horan, Richard Marx, and Latin Pop

Ivan Rakitić

Hometown: Möhlin, Switzerland
Club: FC Barcelona

Born in Switzerland and raised by Croatian parents, Ivan Rakitić decided to play for the national team of his parents' birth, Croatia, despite coming up through the ranks of Swiss soccer. With a father and older brother who were also footballers, Rakitić's interest in the sport was inevitable. But his talent was far from ordinary, and by the age of 16 English side Chelsea was already trying to sign him.

Opting to join local FC Basel's youth program, rather than go to the Premier League, Rakitić remained close to home, learning his craft, and making his senior team debut in September 2005 for the Swiss Super League club. By his second season, he established himself as a regular contributor, scoring 11 goals in 33 Super League matches. He was named the best young player in the league for the 2006–2007 season and soon drew the attention of the larger European clubs who had seen promise in him as a 16-year-old.

Three years older and more experienced, Rakitić signed with Schalke 04 of the Bundesliga in 2007 and debuted in July. He would finish his first season with three goals and 10 assists in 29 games. The year also saw him join Croatia's senior team, for whom he collected one goal in five caps. Playing in the Bundesliga and for Croatia for three-and-a-half seasons, Rakitić emerged as one of the top midfielders in Europe. In 2010 he moved to Sevilla in La Liga. An immediate starter, Rakitić captained Sevilla in 2013–2014 to a Europa League title, during which he scored 15 goals and made 17 assists. Barcelona signed Rakitić in June 2014, where he won a treble his first season and is now an integral part of one of the greatest professional teams in soccer.

Fast Stat:

100

Number of chances Ivan created with Sevilla in 2012–2013, ranking fourth among all players in Europe

Ht: 6'0" • **Wt:** 159 • **DOB:** 3/10/88

Position: Midfield

2015–2016 salary:
$9 million

Career club goals/International caps:
80 goals/81 caps

Twitter: @ivanrakitic

Did you know? Ivan has a tattoo of his brother's name, Dejan, on his right arm.

As a kid: Ivan began his soccer career with hometown club Möhlin-Riburg at the age of four.

Favorite foods: Seville-style fried fish, Catalan tomato-with-bread (*pa amb tomàquet*), and Catalan crème brûlée (*crema catalana*)

Hobbies: Spending time with his Spanish wife, Raquel, and their two daughters, Althea and Adara

Favorite music: Latin pop singer David Bisbal

"I live for football, to be 100 percent, to enjoy it—and to enjoy it you must be at the top of your game."

—Ivan Rakitić

James Rodríguez

Hometown: Cúcuta, Colombia
Club: Real Madrid

Even more impressive than winning the Golden Boot at the age of 23 at the 2014 World Cup (as the tournament's highest goalscorer), is that James Rodríguez managed the feat despite his Colombia team making it only as far as the quarterfinals. On top of that, his goal against Uruguay was chosen by fans as the Goal of the Tournament. Even Argentinian legend Diego Maradona thought Rodríguez should have received the Golden Ball (as the tournament's best player) over his own countryman, Lionel Messi.

Whether scoring goals, dribbling past opponents, or making assists, Rodríguez is a spectacular young attacking midfielder who has burst onto the international stage. Seasoned from the age of 16 first with Colombian side Envigado, then for three years with the Argentine club Banfield, in Portugal with Porto for three more, and in Ligue 1 with Monaco for one, Rodríguez's dazzling performance in the 2014 World Cup led him to a costarring role on the richest club in the world, Real Madrid.

Rodríguez's accomplishments before 2014 were no less impressive. Named the Argentine Primera Division's 2009 Young Player of the Year, the 2011–2012 Primeira Liga Breakthrough Player of the Year with Porto, and AS Monaco Player of the Year for 2013–2014 (as well as Ligue 1's assist leader), Rodríguez also led his Porto team to three straight league titles and a 2011 UEFA Europa League Final victory. Since joining Real Madrid in 2014 and playing alongside the likes of Cristiano Ronaldo and Gareth Bale, he was named to the La Liga Team of the Season for 2014–2015 and posted the highest goals total of his career that year with 17.

Fast Stat:

6

Goals scored by James in five 2014 World Cup matches, most in the tournament

Ht: 5'10" • **Wt:** 172 • **DOB:** 7/12/91

Position: Midfield/Winger

2015–2016 salary:
$15.1 million

Career club goals/International caps:
89 goals/50 caps

Twitter: @jamesdrodriguez

Did you know? James' father, Wilson James Rodríguez, was also a talented footballer, who played for the Colombia national U-20 team.

As a kid: At the age of 11, in Colombia's premier youth tournament, James scored two goals in the final match on corner kicks.

Favorite foods: Bandeja paisa (traditional Colombian dish with red beans, rice, and meat)

Hobbies: Reading (James overcame a childhood stutter by reading books out loud), computers, and spending time with his wife, Daniela Ospina, and their daughter, Salome

Favorite music: Reggaeton

"Diego Maradona, Lionel Messi, Luis Suárez, James Rodríguez—they do things because they have certain gifts that make them special."

—Uruguay manager Óscar Tabárez

"We haven't had a goalscorer like him...for a long time. He is on a different planet to anyone else."

—Former French star Jean-Pierre Papin

Zlatan Ibrahimović

Hometown: Malmö, Sweden
Club: Manchester United

156

Goals Zlatan scored in his last four seasons, more than he did in his previous eight

Ht: 6'5" • **Wt:** 185 • **DOB:** 10/3/81

Position: Striker

2015–2016 salary:
$13.3 million

Career club goals/International caps:
398 goals/116 caps

Twitter: @Ibra_official

Did you know? Zlatan speaks five languages—Swedish, Bosnian, English, Spanish, and Italian.

As a kid: At the age of 15, Zlatan considered quitting soccer to work at the docks in Malmö, but his coach convinced him to stick with it.

Favorite foods: Italian

Hobbies: Taekwondo, movies, video games, and supporting various charitable causes

Favorite music: Reggae, rock, and hip-hop, especially Swedish rapper Timbuktu and Ivorian singer Alpha Blondy

It took less than four years for Zlatan Ibrahimović to become the top goalscorer in Paris Saint-Germain history. Born and raised in Sweden (of Bosnian and Croatian descent), Ibrahimović also rose to the top of team Sweden's career goals list with 62. At the ripe old age of 35, the towering veteran striker seems to be aging more like a fine French wine than a typical footballer—which is probably why in July 2016 he was scooped up by Manchester United, where he's already netted four goals in seven matches.

Growing up in the Swedish port of Malmö, Ibrahimović idolized Brazilian superstar Ronaldo and began playing soccer after receiving his first pair of boots at the age of six. Signing with Malmö FF in 1996 and moving up to the senior side in 1999, Ibrahimović began an itinerant career that would take him to Dutch club Ajax, Italian sides Juventus and Internazionale, Spanish Barça, back to Italy and AC Milan, Paris Saint-Germain and Ligue 1, and finally in 2016 to Manchester United and the Premier League. A consistent offensive threat, the well-traveled Ibrahimović is the only player to have scored for six different clubs in the Champions League. He's been a part of 12 different league champions, is a two-time Ligue 1 Player of the Year, and a four-time Swedish Male Athlete of the Year.

Eligible to play for Bosnia-Herzegovina and Croatia, Ibrahimović chose to play for the country of his birth and represented Sweden from 2001 to his retirement from international play in 2016. Named captain in 2012, he is one of only 10 players to have more than 100 caps with the team. With his powerful ball-striking, agility, and acrobatic ability, he is considered one of the most complete strikers of his generation.

Kevin De Bruyne

Hometown: Drongen, Belgium
Club: Manchester City

One of the best young playmakers in soccer today, at 24 Kevin De Bruyne has already made the rounds of European soccer. After an up-and-down early career, he looks to have come into his own, having excelled in Germany with Wolfsburg and now making an impact with Manchester City.

De Bruyne began his youth career at the age of six with KVV Drongen and made his professional debut at 17 with Genk, scoring six goals and 16 assists for a team that won the Belgian Pro League in 2010–2011. His performance there brought interest from Premier League power Chelsea, who brought him over to West London in 2012. Almost immediately, though, he was loaned out to Bundesliga team Werder Bremen for a year before returning to Chelsea in 2013. A combination of Chelsea's already powerful roster and a knee injury in the fall of 2013 limited De Bruyne's appearances, and he was transferred to Wolfsburg in the Bundesliga in January 2014.

In 2014–2015, his breakout season, De Bruyne scored 16 goals and 27 assists in all matches and was named the 2015 Footballer of the Year in Germany. He began the 2015–2016 season by winning the DFL-Supercup against Bayern Munich with an assist and a goal. On August 30, 2015, Manchester City signed De Bruyne for £55 million, one of highest transfer fees in British soccer history. Joining a Man City lineup featuring Kun Agüero and Yaya Touré, De Bruyne netted 16 goals in his first season. A solid contributor on his Belgium national team, De Bruyne scored against the U.S. in the round of 16 at the 2014 World Cup and was named man of the match versus Algeria. A versatile playmaker and goalscorer, De Bruyne has a bright future.

Fast Stat:

27

Assists Kevin made in all matches with Wolfsburg in 2014–2015

Ht: 5'11" • **Wt:** 150 • **DOB:** 6/28/91

Position: Midfield/Winger

2015–2016 salary:
$9.9 million

Career club goals/International caps:
65 goals/48 caps

Twitter: @DeBruyneKev

Did you know? Kevin broke the record for most assists in a Bundesliga season, with 21 in 2014–2015.

As a kid: Kevin played soccer in the garden of the house his parents built in the village of Drongen (part of the city of Ghent) from the age of three until six.

Favorite foods: Cake

Hobbies: Playstation, baking

Favorite music: Electronic dance music, hip-hop, and R&B

"He has that special footballing instinct that not all players have."

—Wolfsburg sporting director Klaus Allofs

Luis Suárez

Hometown: Salto, Uruguay
Club: FC Barcelona

Fast Stat:

47

Number of goals Suárez has scored in international competition

Ht: 5'11" • **Wt:** 187 • **DOB:** 1/24/87

Position: Striker

2015–2016 salary:
$13.3 million

Career club goals/International caps:
314 club goals/88 caps

Twitter: @LuisSuárez9

Did you know? Luis joined the Groningen club in order to be closer to his childhood sweetheart, Sofia, now his wife, in Barcelona.

As a kid: Luis moved to Montevideo with his family, where he says he really learned to play soccer.

Favorite foods: After biting Giorgio Chiellini at the 2014 World Cup, the joke started on social media that his favorite cuisine was "Italian."

Hobbies: Playing Playstation and spending time with his kids

Favorite music: Latin music

Usually named as one of the top soccer players in the world, Luis Suárez has the distinction of also being recognized as one of the sport's most controversial.

One of eight children, Suárez learned soccer on the streets of the Uruguayan capital of Montevideo, where he also had to work as a street sweeper to help support his family. At the age of 14, Suárez joined the Club Nacional youth team in Montevideo and moved up the ranks to the first team by the time he was 18.

While Dutch club Groningen reps were in Uruguay to scout another player, they saw Suárez play in one game and made an offer to buy him out. Suárez spent one season with Groningen before being bought out by Ajax, where he flourished, scoring 111 goals over four seasons with the Amsterdam club. In 2010 Suárez moved to Liverpool in the Premier League, a £22.8 million signing. In four years there, he netted 82 goals and in 2014 earned the PFA Players' Player of the Year award, Premier League Player of the Year, FWA Footballer of the Year, and shared the European Golden Shoe with Cristiano Ronaldo.

However, Suárez's sometimes questionable tactics have earned him red cards and fan enmity over the years. In the 2010 World Cup he committed a handball in Uruguay's match against Ghana (though it did save the game), and he has bitten three opposing players (the most famous incident occurring in the 2014 World Cup).

Suárez was purchased by Barcelona in 2014 and has scored 92 goals in 106 games for Barça, winning another Golden Shoe in 2015–2016 as La Liga's top scorer.

"He is near unplayable. He on his own can occupy a back four with his movement and his cleverness."

— Liverpool manager Brendan Rodgers

Marco Reus

Thomas Müller

Gareth Bale

Paul Pogba